EDEN THRIVES WITHIN

A Collection of Awakening Poetry

Published by the Natural Being Foundation, 2022

Church House, East Grafton, Marlborough, Wiltshire, SN8 3DB, UK

Email contact: NaturalBeingFoundation@gmail.com

ISBN: 9798834312062 (Paperback)

Copy Editor Rhys Milsom
Cover Image by Amy, Pretty Sleepy Art (Pixabay)
Cover design by Abdul Umar Sahan Nethmina and JMH
Book formatting by Katherine Watkins

First edition 2022

EDEN THRIVES WITHIN

A Collection of Awakening Poetry

by

J.M. Harrison

THE NATURAL BEING FOUNDATION, MARLBOROUGH, UK

Also by J.M. Harrison

We Are All One: A Call to Spiritual Uprising

WINNER - ALL BOOKS INTERNATIONAL EDITOR'S CHOICE AWARD 2009
(Spirituality & Inspiration)

Naked Being: Undressing your Mind, Transforming your Life

FINALIST - USA BOOK NEWS BEST BOOKS AWARD 2010 (Spirituality)

You Are This: Awakening to the Living Presence of Your Soul

The Soul Whisperer: A Tale of Hidden Truths & Unspoken Possibilities

WINNER - 4th ANNUAL BEVERLY HILLS INTERNATIONAL BOOK AWARDS°
(Visionary Fiction 2016)

Listen to This: A Chronicle of Awakening

#1 AUDIOBOOK AT ESTORIES.COM (Body, Mind & Spirit)

CONTENTS

A NOTE OF THANKS

This collection of spontaneous poetry came to life following a Zenways retreat in March, 2022 led by Daizan Roshi, a master in the Rinzai tradition of Zen.

The *Breakthrough to Zen* retreats are designed specifically to create the ideal conditions for you to find your true nature – to find out who you really are (kensho in Japanese). Based on the "group sanzen" format developed by Zen master Shinzan Roshi, together with the dyad work of American teacher, Charles Berner, they create a uniquely powerful combination. The three-day (64hr) retreats are intense and rewarding, with the added benefit of being stabilised and grounded through the "naikan" Zen practices taught by Zen master Hakuin as detailed in the book "Practical Zen".

The retreat was wholesome and solidifying at the deepest level. When it ended, poetry began to flow through me; contemplations of the nature of self, existence, life and death, the sublime, the heartfelt, the paradoxical and the humorous. Day after day insights morphed into short and simple verse, arriving at any time of day or night, and in a variety of circumstances, whether immersed in nature, taking a shower, driving the car, listening to news of war, about to fall sleep, waking up in the night, and experiencing the passing of a family member. In short, everyday life was the catalyst.

It is through such whispers, echoes and reflections of consciousness beyond and beneath the everyday mind that the paradoxical awareness of our true nature can be shared.

This book would not have been possible without the contributions of Rhys, Katherine, Abdul and Amy, so thanks to you all. And thank you to everyone who shared so graciously throughout the retreat, for their openness and generosity in tandem with the support of the Zenways team, helped make it such an illuminating experience.

And finally, I'd like to say a big thank you to Daizan for his unwavering pivotal influence, and to the ordinary-extraordinary that is ... Zen.

May these words serve and inspire you.

JMH 2022

OH, THE CALM OF IT ALL
(Nothing is missing in the
emptiness of things)

Dedicated to D.

In the stateless state,
Nothing is to be known,
For knowingness is like a marksman's arrow
Flying high, seeking an impossible target,
The centre of which is already reached:
This is the pathless path,
The clear, certain paradox.

Here I am
When there is no *self*,
The one placeless place
Where no one *is* and *all* are *living*:
A clear enigma
Completely full of nothing,
Something and everything.

Here, and there, tears turn to laughter
And pleasure turns to pain,
This anonymous true nature
Inseparable from the rotting trodden twig
And the boundless, limitless universe:
The farthest unreachable, here, in the palm of a hand,
Gone and un-leave-able.

This is no trick of the mind or mirage of confusion,
Letting go only renews this infinite luminosity,
Nothing is missing in the emptiness of things,
Walking away leads back here
To the ordinary beyond duality and non-duality:
The choice-less, change-less
Original destination of all things and non-things.

Home is here
At the crossroads, far away in the distance,
A point the mind can never reach
At the destination no one ever leaves,
There's nowhere to go and everywhere to be:
So don't waste a minute, get going now!

Oh!

The calm of it all....

∞

THANK YOU MIND

Thank you, mind,
For falling in line,
For seeing your way
To allow *this* to be.

Thank you, mind,
For being so kind
And for taking it all
So decently.

Thank you, mind,
For not interrupting
No longer disrupting
The naturally free

Thank you, mind,
For all the times
You made me blind
So I could see

Thank you, mind,
For ceding control
By submitting to reason
With *I don't know.*

Thank you, mind,
For falling in line,
For playing your role
And letting *this* be.

∞

ON THIS STILL DAY

On this still day, a tempest is roaring,
In the dark of the night, the sun burns bright,
Peace is here yet war is raging,
How vast the world through a spider's eye?

A lifetime, famished and always hungry,
The relentless fool amasses belongings,
Living a life of death and suffering,
Seemingly found, when lost in things.

Eternity breathes as chaos lingers,
For fixed opinions are stubbornly blind,
Wake in the night to infinity's knowing
That clinging to God is a waste of time.

On this still day, a tempest is roaring,
Listen, do you hear?
Look, can you see?
Shake your mind and eternity arises,
Here, now,
Reality.

∞

MY DOG HAS BUDDHA NATURE

Dedicated to R.

My dog has Buddha Nature, there is no doubt
He helps me and talks with loving eyes,
He even thinks of me when I'm out.

My dog has Buddha Nature, he watches attentively,
And when it's time to go to bed,
It's my wife, the Buddha and me.

My dog has Buddha Nature, he's lying beside me now,
Pure and true, transparent and free,
But still the blind look and just don't see.

My dog has Buddha Nature, he's wise evidently,
He knows what to do, how to communicate
And *just* how to be.

My dog has Buddha Nature, he's barking
away right now,
Telling the noisy ones outside,
To stop disturbing the peace he's found.

My dog has Buddha Nature, he's natural and free,
He's a teacher, an explorer,
And he walks beside me.

My dog has Buddha Nature; now do you
understand me?
If you can't grasp what I'm saying
Then keep on practicing until you see

My dog has Buddha Nature; do you think it
can't be true?
For if you don't see Buddha in everything,
You're missing the real in you.

My dog has Buddha Nature, and if *you* want to be free,
Don't take your life so personally,
Just stop thinking,
And be.

∞

NOT ME, NOT-NOT ME

Face your pain, devour it
Or leave it to fester,
Touching the source
Resolves all suffering,
For as the snow melts, the sun dies
And *all* remains strong and true.

I can't take your pain away,
If your ego desires
To manifest shadows,
Seek your nature
And your death will set you free
As sure as the river is full of dry stone.

Take your pain away?
Oh, if only I could,
Then we'd be together as one,
Where we've always been
Not me,
Not-not me.

∞

INFINITY HERE NOW

This true gentle heart,

Discovered in a bird's song

On a timeless morning

Of ordinary limitless joy,

Soft and intimate thoughtlessness,

Solid and still

Rushing like water,

The whole in the part,

Infinity,

Here, now.

∞

CAUGHT IN A CANDLE

Hot wax, dripping,
Cold stone, up
There, down there,
All here,
Appearance, motion and stillness
Are but one.

Locked away in this
Boundless freedom,
Imprisoned by nature, free
To leave in any moment,
Gratefully stuck, fast.

Only sightseers leave,
For all travels
begin and end here.
Rejoice!
Life's heavenly jail
Awaits,
Each timeless moment.

∞

THE BLISS OF THE UNKNOWN

I cannot seek for what is here
In words, in music, in stillness,
Fruitlessly grasping for the emptiness
Of solid, intimate love.

I cannot find what is here
Yet here it remains, everywhere,
Within my breath,
At the heart of a golden sun.

I cannot leave what is here,
Beyond word and thought,
Being the limitless universe
Inside the pip of an apple.

I cannot name what is here
Where nothing needs to be known,
For all is lost and found
In the bliss of the unknown.

∞

GONE TO THE DOGS

Out and about, nowhere, in a pack of wolves,
Famished not feeding,
Walking not talking,
Just *being* not thinking.

Out and about, nowhere, in a pack of wolves,
Lost in eternity's game,
Happiness is our prey,
A guiltless kill in every way.

Out and about, nowhere, in a pack of wolves,
Just over here in the shallow depths of it all
Seeing the dead, trapped by bones,
Cradled in the smile of a hunter.

Out and about, nowhere, in a pack of wolves
In this un-breathable air,
Lungs fill with the sweetest of nothings,
Here the found is re-found, and found again,
Out and about, nowhere, in a pack of wolves.

∞

LETTING GO

The practice of letting go
Leads to letting go
Of all things -
Let go now -
It's *all* going to go, anyhow,
So let it go.

If you continue letting go,
Your mask will fall,
Revealing the original face in all,
Just remove your disguise,
It only hides the beauty inside
So let it go.

When you've found the secret -
Let it go -
With nowhere left to roam,
When all doubts resolve
In I don't know,
Carry on,
Let it go.

When the found is choiceless being-

Let it go -

As metal and magnet unite as one

And you a carefree child become,

When all such wonders have been and gone,

Just carry on,

Let it go.

∞

A NATURAL STORM

The fool clings tight
As the sage drowns in a sea of emptiness,
Both living, and dying.

The fool marvels at his survival
As the sage drinks from a bottomless ocean,
The fool boasts of his remarkable journey
While the eyes of the sage twinkle with light.

The fool's fear returns,
still scared and frightened of life
As the sage devours death
With a relentless thirst.

The fool yearns to be as free
As the sage *is*
And someday
He will be.

∞

CALM LOVE

Calm Love, Calm Love
Everything is one
Calm Love, Calm Love
Not my one
Calm Love, Calm Love
Not two
Calm Love, Calm Love
Limitless view
Calm Love, Calm Love
Utterly blind
Calm Love, Calm Love
All is nothing
Calm Love, Calm Love
Infinite drops of metal rain
Calm Love, Calm Love

∞

I AM NOTHING, NOTHING, NOTHING

In the depths of creation
Beyond worldly knowledge:
I am *nothing, nothing, nothing.*

Gorging on bread and water
At the infinite feast in an unknowable kingdom:
I am *nothing, nothing, nothing.*

Aqua like gold, so fulfilling
It pours from my mouth, overflowing:
I am *nothing, nothing, nothing.*

Crystalline mind, empty and full,
Beyond pinnacles and miracles:
I am *nothing, nothing, nothing.*

Founder of the universe,
Sounder of the spheres:
I am *nothing, nothing, nothing.*

God's voice gone,
Being here:
I am *nothing, nothing, nothing.*

Laughter-less bliss beyond words,
All missing in absence:
I am *nothing, nothing, nothing.*

Nothing I think,
Really is:
I am *nothing, nothing, nothing.*

All that remains
Is the nothing I am,
Nothing, nothing, nothing.

∞

THE HEART OF THIS
UNGRASPABLE NOWHERE

At the heart
Of this ungraspable nowhere
Sits no-one,
Safely secured by implausible chains
Of paper-like stone.

Never to leave
Eternity's jail -
Peaceful -
Timeless presence,
Realm-less and indivisible.

Here, the doer is done,
And being can but *be* -
At the heart of this
Ungraspable,
Nowhere.

∞

TO CLING

To cling to ego
Means you'll never win,
To cling to power,
Weakness brings.

To cling to joy,
Beckons pain,
To cling to the sun,
Only brings the rain.

To cling to light,
Ensures darkness will come,
To cling to right,
Only proves you are wrong.

To cling to love,
Allows for hate,
Cling to life
And death awaits.

To cling to winning
Is a loser's game,
Cling to freedom
And the prisoner remains.

Cling to Buddha
And enlightenment's gone,
So cling to nothing
Then clinging is done.

∞

STILLNESS RUNS FREE

Seeing the beech tree
As home, as shelter,
Spotting the robin
Sat preening one wing,
Watching the wind,
A thousand leaves dancing -
At the heart of it all,
Stillness runs free.

Writing words
No one has spoken,
Watching the clouds
Float purposefully,
Hearing the news,
Somebody's speaking
Opinions and views -
As stillness runs free.

Planning the day
Long since forgotten,
Following the way
Of nature's reality,
Born to a world of something and nothing
Where the living are fading -
As stillness runs free.

All waves rise up as the ocean,
The shape of the shingle is forged by the sea,
Here stands somebody,
The appearance of someone,
When beneath all someone's,
Stillness runs free.

What's the true cost of living
When life has been gifted so generously?
Find truth
Always within you,
Let yourself go
And stillness runs free,
Just let go
And stillness runs free

∞

PARADOX OF THE UNIFIED MIND

Wandering away
Leads back here,
Where peace abides
And clinging to nothing
Abandons all notions of things,
Puerile tales of the once-was
Fade into obscurity.

In the anonymous here and gone
With egos mirage stripped
Helpless and bare,
Limitless peace springs
Impossibly now
Above a groundless Earth
Here below
Within, beyond the *Tao*.

One is one,
Both vast and small,
Eternity's heart
Resounds
Through all.

∞

CHANGELESS

Dwelling in choices
Brings discrimination,
Opulence and affluence
Set no-one free.

The mystic draws triangular circles in the sand
And sees through the world
Escaping nothing,
Accepting everything.

When changeless is found,
Changeless *is*.

Changeless you,
Changeless me,
Only the changeless
May truly be.

∞

INVISIBLE KNOWN

Intellectual prisoners
Endlessly debate their nature,
While ego's folly
Is believing 'I know'
Negating nothing
From every direction,
All laid bare:
Invisible,
Known.

∞

THIS SELF

I have always been
This Self,
A saint and a sinner,
A patient and a healer.

Never anyone but
This Self,
Lost and found,
Chained and unbound.

Nothing to see here but
This Self,
Invisible to no-one,
Only one, everyone.

All seeing is
This Self,
Knowing not proven,
Awareness unspoken.

Beyond Kabbalah
Is This Self,
Buddha and Christ,
Krishna and Father.

Timeless love
Is This Self,
Near and distant,
The source of existence.

All I've ever been
Is This Self,
Both good and bad,
The sane and mad.

Nothing transcends
This imminent Self,
Disguised or covered,
Fathered and mothered.

Nothing *is*
Other than This Self,
Peaceful knowing
Everything's flowing
For all is nothing
But This
Self.

∞

HERE AND GONE

The mountain melts
The ice cold sun
As light and dark unveil as one,
Serenity sings
The sweetest song
Yet, I am,
Here and gone.

Old ghosts once lived,
Re-magnify anew,
Avoiding nothing,
Nature's coup,
Purpose and Dharma,
Empty as one
Yet, I am,
Here and gone.

Deaf to the lure of
The sirens' call,
Lost in the infinite
Self in all,
Ever and always,
Present all along
And yet, I am,
Here and gone.
Yet, I am
Here,
Gone.

∞

NO-THING IS AS IT SEEMS

No-thing
Is
As it seems.

For I am
You
And you are, too.

When there *is* no me
And there *is* no you,
Only one inextricable
Truth.

No-thing
Is
As it seems.

∞

THE BUDDHA IN ME

A sage speaks words of
wisdom -
That's the Buddha in me -

The crazy man chatters,
no one understands -
That's the Buddha in me -

Serious laughter, knowing
suffering, loving life to death -
That's the Buddha in me -

Each someone being no-one -
That's the Buddha in me -

Consistently contradictory
and always true -
That's the Buddha in me -

Walking, meditating,
practicing, contemplating,
silence, peace, joy -
That's the Buddha in me -

Being and doing -
That's the Buddha in me -

Surrendering in each and
every moment -
That's the Buddha in me -

Telling my wife I love her -
That's the Buddha in me -

Explaining to a daughter
she's free -
That's the Buddha in me -

Smiling without words -
That's the Buddha in me -

A reminder of what can
never leave -
That's the Buddha in me -

A maggot crawls out of a hole
in a perfectly bruised apple -
That's the Buddha in me –

While the universe blinks -
That's the Buddha in me -

Unborn, undying, accepting
the richness of imperfection -
That's the Buddha in me -

Home here and far away -
That's the Buddha in me -

No-one else to be
The Buddha in me.

∞

INEVITABLY

The hottest sun
Invites the heaviest rain
And arid deserts
Lead to the deepest seas –
When thinking deciphers
The real and true,
Then you are lost,
Inevitably

As sure as everything
Is really nothing
And the awakened
Will no-one be -
Looking for secrets
Mistakenly seeking,
Then you are lost,
Inevitably

From restlessness
Comes serenity

In knowing this
The paradox runs free –
All our yesterdays
Turn into tomorrows
And you are lost,
Inevitably.

Holding truth
Between your fingers,
Allowing to forget and see
When life appears
Beyond mind's reason,
Then you are lost,
Inevitably.

When you find
God's mind within you
And life flows
Unquestionably,
Seeing through the once imagined,
Then you are lost,
Inevitably.

By confusing those around you
Nestled in life's clarity,
No-one knows the truth
You're living
For you are lost,
Inevitably.

When life unfolds
In endless beginnings,
When love gives love,
Transforming hate,
When all is found
In finding nothing,
Then you are lost,
Inevitably.

∞

WASH ME AWAY

Wash me away, wash me away,
Zephyr of the universe,
Wash me away.

Wash me away, wash me away,
Invisible nameless serenity,
Wash me away.

Wash me away, wash me away,
Joyful entirety,
Wash me away.

Wash me away, wash me away,
So nothing is left,
Wash me away

Wash me away, wash me away
In silence and peace
Wash me away

Wash me away, wash me away,
Oh, single soul,
Wash me away.

Wash me away, wash me away,
One into one,
Wash me away.

Wash me away, wash me away,
Without and within,
Wash me away.

Wash me away, wash me away,
Until all I was is no more,
Wash me away.

∞

WHEN YOU ARE GONE

When you are gone,
You are here,
When your body has given up the ghost,
You are here.

When your mind no longer plays the host,
You are here,
Where else could you be?
There is no 'other' than eternity.

There is no leaving
For anyone, in truth,
You are here
When you are gone.

A gentle word
To all who grieve,
You cannot miss
What never leaves.

Just ask the ether
And morning dew
For you are in them
And they, are you.

∞

YOU ALL ALONG

Dedicated to R

Do not cling to life
As if this world is the be-all and the end,
Breathe deep and let yourself go
For, in the fullness of time
Life and death are *something* and *nothing*

Climb, striven soul,
Your immortal home awaits
Where perfect peace resides
In love, everlasting.

No more needs
And no more regrets,
Only blameless remains
Litter a path well-trodden.

Just know this one thing...
I was you, all along.

∞

A HERD OF EARTHLY GHOSTS

Lifetimes are spent
Manifesting all these earthly ghosts,
Only to drown
In the quietus of truth,
Then, to return,
Finding your way,
Once more
To the light of day.

What shall become of you
In fear of life, avoiding truth?
The deluded grasp inherited beliefs,
Only bringing transient relief,
Fading with each passing moment
Egos feign, slobber and boast,
Rushing headlong, nowhere fast,
This vanishing herd
Of earthly ghosts.

∞

SAFELY LOST IN THE HEART OF IT ALL

Safely lost
In the heart of it all,
Where no eye can see
And nothing befalls.

No one to need,
No one to be,
Nothing to crave,
No one to free,
Nothing to find
And no place to go.

Celestial whispers
Resound through invisible walls
In this,
Our Elysian Home.

∞

THE PARADOX OF THE FREE

In a timeless moment,
Free to be something
And nothing.

Filled,
Complete and lacking,
Found,
When all about is lost.

No-one to save,
For death is birth's destiny,
While existence is eternity
In this simple knowing
The here and gone
Live free.

∞

MANIMAL

Oh, Manimal,
Lost in the ramblings
Of oblivion
And addicted to the pleasures
Of your selfish discontent,
Aimlessly wandering
The mind's mirages,
Wallowing in the nausea
Of the ego's masquerade.

A poor, vain, foolish actor
Portraying a pointless
Non-existent role.

Oh, Manimal,
What a trail you blaze
In your world of fakery -
Truth lies misplaced.

Blind to all harm done,
Lost in the miasma
You've become,
No imagery can truly hide
The emptiness you feel inside.

Oh, Manimal,
Look what you've become,
Slipping back to animal,
Not blossoming human
And yet, all is not lost
For should you turn,
Rise and climb,
Your mind will soar
To the un-thought heights
Of a golden paradigm.

∞

NATURE'S MANIFEST

When *doing*
Is innocuous as a robin's breath
And life is
Flowing ceaselessly,
Discourse at rest,
When 'others' fade
At Awakening's behest:
Nature's
Manifest.

When the shadows
Cause is clear as light
And fear has lost
Its soulless fight,
You wake and sleep
Alive and bright:
Nature's
Manifest.

Not the special,
Not the foe
Drawn together,
Essence be-known,
You are the lone
And all the rest:
Nature's
Manifest.

Eyes ablaze,
What not who,
No-one, some-one
Living true
In each moment
Life renews:
Nature's
Manifest.

∞

ONCE A LION

Holding head in hand
As the fading child
Stumbles his way home,
Once a lion
Roaring chaos, grunting pain,
Now a choiceless infant
Tapping on eternity's door.

Nothing and no-one
Is found to forgive -
I love you -
Thank you for being who you are -
These few simple words,
Are the heartfelt farewell
To the pitiful child,
Once a lion.

∞

I AM UNDONE

No, not I,
No banging the drum,
Those days are done and over,
No one's left here to succumb.

Eternity's opportune rhythm
Followed by no-one,
Sounds her deafening silence,
Nature's unwavering song.

Secretly dancing
To life's endless beat,
Deep, flowing like rain,
Singing in the light.

In the world,
But not of it,
With no other to become,
Choice-less,
Freedom plays her tune
And I, I am
Undone.

∞

CHANGELESS

The weather
Comes and goes
While the sky
Remains
Always.

The mind of ego
Is but a shadow
In the light
Of the one
Selfless sun.

When shadows fade,
Consciousness
Shines unhindered
In timeless moments,
With no-one to deny
The undeniable.

When the clouds of doubt
Clear away,
All that remains
Is the one sun,
In the one blue sky.
Just as when the mask of the self is lifted
And confusion is unravelled and done,
All you will be
Is the nameless
Presence, nobody
Can become.

∞

NOMAD MIND

Here, clothed
In cumbersome guise,
Wandering a world
Of ghosts and dreams.

No preference
Comes to mind,
Not offended
By any kind.

In this moment,
No-one remains to be defended,
Surrendering to life,
Captivity ended.

Safely home
I roam the flowing haven
Of this -
Nomad mind.

∞

WITHIN

Is that you,
Faceless God?
In asking,
Such questions
Dissolve into oblivion,
Yet still,
Nature sings
Her timeless truth,
Serenading each new day
With melodies of natural joy,
Precise and clear,
Notes of comfort to someone
And no-one's ear.

Joyful are those
Who realise
These songs
of earthly paradise,
Appearing on the outside
Arise from us,
Within.

∞

MINDLESS SUNSHINE

In the river of life,
I lose myself,
Flowing in all.

Mindless words,
Gifts of impetus
Revealing oneness,
Unblocking karma,
Unlocking Nirvana.

Idioms fall like celestial rain,
Un-blamed, unnamed
And unashamedly
Bringing sunshine
To none and all.

Wanting turns to allowing
Transcending claims of creation
And narration.

In such crystalline moments,

No questions are found,

Words appear

In absence of doubt

For with the mind flowing,

Still and quiet,

The sun is always out.

∞

THIS ONE AND ALL

Always here, life
Is not trying to get somewhere,
Already *everyone*,
It has no desire to be *someone*.

As the everything it is, was
And will be,
The seeking of otherness
Only fashions fruitless vanities,
Demi-dreams that whittle away
To their lifeless beginnings.

This unchanging effortless flow,
This sole indivisible faithless truth
Is the most obvious, unrecognised secret,
The imminent, infinite
Presence of all.

And when you are ripe,

You will drop

And *rise*, not fall,

Flowing as nature's intended

For *we* are

This,

One and All.

∞

UNBORN

Dedicated to Bankei.

Re-claimed through aura,
Re-formed into matter -
It's genesis,
No 'I' can see.

Unborn, undying,
No-one's will,
In heaven's Gomorrah,
Running free.

Beyond the senses,
Neither encouraging nor preventing,
The inborn is the unborn
Verity.

∞

THE BENUMBED

Names and titles,
Meaningless rhymes,
Countries and kingdoms,
Biased designs.

Wealth and power,
Reeking like thieves,
Fake politicians,
Recycling deceit.

TV and media,
Pumping out shit,
Comatose minds,
Accepting it.

Scattering madness,
Fear and despair,
The snore of the benumbed,
Fills the air.

Lost in the world,
No-one fully lives,
While pushing away,
Life ceaselessly gives.
So stand up, rise up,
Awakening's at hand,
Nirvana is here
In the heart-mind
Of Man.

∞

YOULESS

Not the seeker
But the sought -
Not the thinker,
Not the thought -
Within the part
Ever the sole
Sacred heart of nature's whole.

Nothing to prove,
With nothing to lose -
Nothing to hinder or confuse,
Arising from nowhere
Beyond space and time,
This *you-less* presence:
One infinite mind.

∞

SELF-PORTRAIT

The art of the Self paints life

True

On a clear canvas unimpeded by

You.

∞

A FRUITFUL LIFE

A fruitful life,
Lived and breathed,
Embraces suffering and disease
And laughter, love and ecstasy.

Vicissitudes
Such as these
Allow us all to fully see
The gifts of balance and harmony.

For the soul, untethered
From all such things,
Lives fruitful and free
And by nature, sings.

∞

ONE BUT NONE

Opinions choke
And egos blame,
Seeking difference
To self-inflate
While life unfolds
Nature's way -
We are One,
But none.

Through love and war,
Her mystery runs,
A formless heart
No-one becomes,
Discarding the veil
Illusion succumbs -
For we are One,
But none.

Inhabiting a world of form and change,
Overlooking the dustless
Whence we came,
The shimmering light
In all remains -
We are One,
But none.

∞

AT THE HEART OF IT ALL

In sadness,
Rain falls
Just like tears.

In happiness
The sun shines bright
Smiles of joy,
In doubt,
Clouds gather to
Face their predicament
In pain and anger,
Storms, lightning
And thunder.

The peaceable awoken,

Accept and acknowledge

All types of weather

Without preference,

Knowing life

Is not lived

By a who

Great or small

But by the *what*

At the heart

Of it all.

∞

AWAKENED BE

If all the world
Awakened be
Flowing in
Reality,
The dying will live
And the blind will see,
When all awakened *be.*

If humankind
Awakened be
Inhabiting
Life's integrity,
War will end
Unequivocally,
When all awakened *be.*

If humanity
Awakened be
Consciously flowing
In dimensions free,
Eyes will know and minds will see,
When all awakened *be.*

∞

EDEN THRIVES WITHIN

When life appears resigned to fate
And problems appear to escalate,
You overlook your inborn state
For Eden thrives within.

When envy rears its ugly head
And your bruised ego's all upset,
Caught in slumber, you forget:
Eden thrives within.

When joyful memories fade away
Returning to the everyday,
Speak these words aloud and say:
Eden thrives within.

When suffering comes back yet again
And fortune reaches the deadest-end
Recall this simple truth, my friend:
Eden thrives within.

∞

THIS BLOSSOMING DIVINE

Across the fields,
golden flowers
are luminous,
bearing gossamer,
sublime
as far as the eye can see,
unveiling nature's *unity*.

I reach across,
touching petals
and tears fall,
in reverence I sigh
at such oneness in abundance
before me.

While no one told these flowers
Nor did they decide,
they live and breathe
the truth of life,
this blossoming
divine.

∞

THE UNTRUE

All that stands
in the way of truth
is the untrue
me
and the untrue
you
for when the untrue
is undone,
the self is lost,
and all
is *one*.

∞

HEART STREAM ETERNAL

There is one, only one
indivisible myriad -
billions –
but one
surpassing creation and oblivion.

This infinite presence
of rich and poor
in *Ra* and dew
flows ever-more.
Intimate anonymity
transcending all dualities -
crystalline –
running free, this
heart-stream eternal.

∞

DESTINY UN-DONE

Jealousy and fear only
Separate,
while love and compassion
amalgamate,
knowing this dismisses fate:
destiny un-done.

Through pride and envy,
aimlessly stray
or follow the course
of nature's way,
let go, the mind of everyday:
destiny un-done.

All that makes you feel at one
mirrors the truth from whence you came,
when mind, just as space becomes:
destiny un-done.

Life gives you but one thing to do,
to walk your path, transparent and true,
illuminating the original you:
destiny un-done.

∞

NAMELESS QUIDDITY

Heavenly breath
brushes a cheek
as golden rays
diffuse the deep,
all-pervading,
ever-free:
nameless quiddity.

To be the heart,
first lose your tale
and leave behind
old, aimless trails,
for peace is found here,
within:
nameless quiddity.

Life's greatest treasures
are to know
who you are
and where is home,
in knowing these
you will be:
nameless quiddity.

∞

I AM YOU

Within this breath,
is life,
vast and small,
part and whole.

One nature living
as star and leaf
and behind the mind
which dies to see

beyond brain, beyond mind,
beyond space, beyond time,
transcending the seen
and formless face.

I am whole:
one, many,
indivisible, true,
I am this,
I am life,
I am you.

∞

THE LANGUAGE OF THE WAY

These words are not my words,
they are songs
heard, unheard
distant airs,
beneath the breath,
awakening's berceuse.

This lucidity
transparently shares
sublime echoes, celestial airs,
the timeless calling
me to you
and for you
to care.

Words are newly-born each day,
their melodies falling
like sacred rain,
transcending joy,
accepting pain,
this language
of *The Way*.

∞

ENDLESS AND ONE

There is no end
to the never-begun,
for love is un-created
by anyone.

In the leaf and the star,
in the piece and the sum
breathes existence:
endless and one.

∞

ESSENCE

Clothed in the myriad of things,
essence flourishes
at the heart of multiplicity,
in childlike whispers,
I am gone, merged
with the light of eternity's song.

More than body,
greater than mind,
surpassing gender, colour and kind,
before all countries, kingdoms and clans,
is essence
which never began.

∞

MUSIC OF NOTE

Isn't it funny
how you, they, and we
are simply *notes*
within life's symphony?

When in tune,
played naturally and free,
our lives flow by
harmoniously.

Yet should the notes
to ego succumb,
it pains the ears
of everyone.

So a melodious mind
will always be,
in unison with
life's symphony.

∞

I LOVE ME TOO

Dedicated to W.

You say you love *me*
And I do love *you*
Yet such dualities
Conceal a broader truth -
For we are indivisible
Just as rain and dew,
Which is why I reply:
"I love me, too."

∞

ABOUT THE AUTHOR

J.M. Harrison (Jonathan) is a consciousness facilitator and founder of The Natural Being Foundation. An award- winning and Amazon#1 author, he began writing following a mystical death experience in 2007. The author of six published books to date, including one audiobook and a collection of awakening poems, he is also an award-winning musician (Gold Disc, 1990, UK).

As a featured presenter on the World Changing Wisdom webinar series, Jonathan taught alongside Barbara Marx-Hubbard, Greg Braden, Barbara Rother, Eric Pearl and others:

http://www.worldchangingwisdom.com/ pastpresenters.html

With extensive media experience, Jonathan has been interviewed on numerous podcasts and radio shows in the US, as well as an interview on Conscious TV: http://conscious.tv/single.php?vid=978419418001

As an elder for *More To Life* he is a regular contributor contributes to the UK's most popular MBS enlightenment magazine https://moretolifemag.co.uk/

Via the non-profit organisation *The Natural Being Foundation,* Jonathan offers complimentary monthly Zoom talks or satsang for those seeking their most intimate and complete sense of Self. If you would like to take part, please contact:

NaturalBeingFoundation@gmail.com

THE NATURAL BEING FOUNDATION

FREE SATSANG VIA ZOOM THE FIRST SUNDAY OF EVERY MONTH

"To seek is to suffer. To seek nothing is bliss."

—Bodhidharma

Printed in Great Britain
by Amazon

82091309R00058